Eggshells &
Entropy

Love Poems

to

Madness & Misanthropy

by
Jace Paul

Copyright © 2013

ART APERITIF BOOKS

Putnam, CT

Library of Congress Cataloging-in-Publication Data

Paul, Jace

Eggshells & Entropy (Love poems to madness and misanthropy) / Jace Paul

ISBN 978-1-304-08105-6

1. Literature – Poetry – I. Title

First edition. Printed in the United States of America.

Cover image: "Where I Began," © 2013 Jace Paul

Table of Contents

The Poems

An Assent
(And Not Quite an Acknowledgment)

My foremost indebtedness goes to Andover-Newton Theological School and Harvard University's Divinity School. It's said that you cannot put a value on education but the fine folks over at the Department of Education and Sallie Mae loan servicing do not agree, and so the debt I would like to declare is very literal, a sum of about $97,000.00. An asset to them, but of course from my point of view this expense - for three utterly useless Master's degrees - is an astounding liability. So, thanks ANTS and HDS for nearly one hundred thousand dollars less than nothing, and increasing the odds that I will die a starving artist.

Oh, all right. Studying religion and philosophy may have been a critical financial blunder on my part but, yes, I did get a lot of writing done and, yes, the arcane scraps of knowledge I picked up along the way may have buffed up my poetry a mote or so. Thus - "thanks," ANTS and HDS. Keep sending me those capital campaign appeal letters and, on the day my degrees make me one penny of income, I'll pitch in to match.

A genuine acknowledgment of gratitude goes to to my friends and family who (more or less) support my choice to exist in abject poverty for the sake of art. Additional gratitude to Paul DuPuis, cleric of the Celtic Orthodox Church (I didn't know either) for his lively tutelage in advanced French grammar, to *The Harvard*

Wick for showcasing "A Tikrit Carol" in their 2008 Fall edition, and to Barbara DeCew, mentor, painter and sculptor, best friend, and source of the true story that inspired "Greg."

At the time of this writing, the most successful book of poems ever published came from pop singer Jewel – not Robert Frost, not Maya Angelou, not Seamus Heaney or Sylvia Plath. Whether that's good or bad is up to you to decide, but I think a minimum standard for artistic success is that *someone* sees the final product. So if you're reading this, my sincerest thanks rightly belongs to you.

Jace Paul

April 2013

For Kristin -

Somewhere there is a universe where we're together,

and in it strange and amazing things: Guinness cupcakes,

much Doctor Who memorabilia, two pairs of lightsaber

chopsticks, a farmhouse abutting Sebet's stable and abundant

prowling space for the cats, a List of Things We Must Do,

a playroom for two smart and beautiful children, two gaming

authenticators, matching Harvard hats, a hiking trail to the top of Old
Furnace, a New England foliage tour, an

engagement ring, and a spread of five happy decades.

If you find yourself lost in time and space,

I'm waiting for you there.

Rain of Ashes

The journey of the magi led them to a birth; renewal

We like to interject, historically.

Somehow faith is not quite innocent.

Any good Christian can espouse the noble   language

Of grace, and love, and all the things that God is, -

More often we hack at each other with words

Always at the ready to draw a neighbor down.

Is it for the sake of absolutism? Is it for better sleep - - -

On the backs of others whose sin is always greater than ours?

Better sleep.

That's a cop out. Really, God got it wrong

We are not beings of light, always striving for higher places

Look at our faces: worn ragged with hate

To kill, to judge, to rob the joy of life and

- no lies -

Exhaust faith until it becomes another excuse for violence

A compulsory sludge in a communal trough
The best poison.

"Sunday morning, Hezbollah in Northern Lebanon. "

Here, two thousand years out from the fable of a
prophet

Self-banished in stupor and tears

Murderers, liars, the worst kind of crooks

Still animals, slaves of more complicated
destinies;

Still absent from the table after all these years.

That Dragonfly Painting In The Bathroom

Day one,
I stepped out of the shower and there it was:
Awful, that dragonfly painting on the wall
Fighting with the paisley wallpaper over who is tackier,
I curled my lip and raised an eyebrow thinking
How could any mother have such poor taste?

Day two,
Dripping wet, I regarded the cruel vision once again
Marveling at the artists disdain for harmony
The childlike brush strokes, scribbles, SCRIBBLES!
Wishing I could toss out this quaint relic of the garish Sixties;
Dried off and dressed for the afternoon picnic.

Day three,
Pulled back the curtain to my lapsed friendship,
There I was. Packing for the trip back home, I asked

May I take that dragonfly painting in the bathroom
with me?

Outside in the neighbors driveway,

a boy flew his basketball at the hoop and missed;
picked it up and tried that must have third time.

A perfect shot!

The Hollow Face

I dropped the tokens in the slot,
And made my way out of the station
Determined to get the first cup of coffee
At the little bakery near home.

Graveyard shift. Why the hell did
I take it? That factory floor did
My soul *in*, a killing machine,
My soul *is* slurry in that machine.

The tunnels were barren. Stark
and silent save the whir of fluorescent lamps.
I wished anyone else were down there
With me. And there it was.

A face, blurred but evidently porcine,
Staring at me from behind a decorative
Pane of frosted glass.

Eggshells & Entropy

I could make out no features except the eyes,
Calm and unblinking. It occurred to me

That it must be another early morning worker.
But there was another sound in the ammonia air
A kind of clicking, muttering, damning
Chant, coming from the hollow face.

And then it stopped, fast as I understood it;
The lamps stopped, and I stopped, too.

And then it squealed; I squealed too.

My feet were pounding the concrete and minutes later
Without a glance back, I was on the street.

The event was easily dismissed
After a day of sleep
As the product of a taxing night and caffeine
withdrawal.

Still there are moments on the hot dog factory floor

That I am certain I see

A squealing, hollow face

Unblinking in the lines of machinery.

A2M

he wrestled with the ascent.   Honestly,
Its not with ease that an old man
Of eighty-four can surmount the craggy
crevasse, skirt outcrops of hair, a scrubland

In the slim air his breathing was labored,
it was hot, humid, and petroleum
Loomed in the air.
But he had come so near.

> (*don't ask where he escaped from but
> just accept that it was a long and
> difficult journey. and it was his time to
> say what he had learned.*)

A long shaft in one hand,
A sagely sorcerer discharging Old Crow when he
exhaled
he stepped over beer cans and discarded
condoms in the din,
undaunted as he sallied on the Brown Trail.

He had the provisional eyes of a crackpot
visionary.

The glassiness and an oak leaf imprint in his
pupils,

and gaze that looked over and beyond and never
focused on anything genitally.

With hazy optics that he surveyed the valley
once visited in youth

A bluff that patronized an ocean of lemony smog
and swimmin'y cars.

From the long jacket he wore he produced -

a severed page from Romans.

He sucked (in) and puffed (up) his chest to
release the ejaculation

calling on the confidence of a modest violet
soused,

Sexuality is a God-given right!

So says Steinem and Joyce Carol Oates.

Fear not the plague of HIV

Lest we become Midianites and our genitals go on.

here he paused to swig from the bottle

What we've done with scriptural inferences,
It's so much flap-doodle,
You can't hang on to mitzvots
Like you can to a noodle.

here he waggled his dick

If you consider the physiological cost of loving,
all those endorphins and the steroids
and the resolution - well then sex is a relationship
laconic!
Have sex to save time!

Suddenly he perceived that he was all alone.

A would-be mentor on top of a mountain and in a closet, fastened.

What kind of fireball is this, bluster and prosody?

He turned. The trail home was littered with broken walls

Where false faces were exhausted and failed
But upon reaching home again,
he took that scatological scepter to mass
And inserted it into the monsignor's maw.

There Are Too Many Kids in This Closed Universe

There are too many elbows
And too many knees,

Could someone create
Some entropy
Please?

Vet Cemetery

I made a business date with the cemetery: 9AM
Sunday.

The realization that sex and violence were
cinnamon and sugar

Pressed me to wanderlust, so, in the rows of
absolutes

Where ancient sepulchers had struck the ground
with a heavy bass note

as risible as the tablets of the Law of Moses:

I went.

Among god's only blameless soldiers, the blades
of grass,

Vigilant in their watch on the history of death,

It seemed that cupped palms make a seamless
gutter for the blood of original sins,

Ivory hands that flip from steeples to fists
wantonly

At the instant religious foment skips the fork in
the narrow way.

Relativism on $5.00 a Day

To maintain a gaze with the void,

reselect your world interface each morning.

Gnosticism will only get you locked away,

Get a latté instead.

Go out in business casual and kiss the feet of
Heaven, or Hell.

There's no difference.

In the gaps you may insert a truth that appeals,

Morality is your affinity for one flavor or
another

And when all is said and done,

few will know, fewer will care:

Vanilla or cheesecake, socialism or slave
morality.

Did you really eat a microwave burrito for lunch?

Fuck no, it was a salad.

Did you dry up in a cubicle when Iphianassa came
to teach?

No, you spent the day with Superman, who
doted on your dithyrambs.

All bets are on.

God(s/ess/esses) will care, or not, depending on your fancy.

You've got a lot less time than a rock to render what suits you,

Followed by grit and coffin, damn all.

The prophet and the *gendarme couché*,

Share nonexistence in perfect harmony

And thus your budget should take account:

A pocket edition of any Tolstoy book is $5

And so is a really good beer.

Sine Qua Non

I split myself this morning
putting away knives.
I paused to let the blood scramble out,
And in one liminal minute
The light show, the fanfare, lasers and fog
Went dead, and god was goddess.

She was unconquerable again on the throne usurped
By over-endowed bulls; mighty and concordant
Behind the scenes. Resplendent in silver, silk,
Ambrosia, she offered a goblet of tears
- not blood!
for making
All things new.

As I drank she turned, and was all at once and always
A chambermaid delighted to arrange,
Prone and in minimal linen
Undiminished for all who stoke apathy.

I hoped to be a bird on her shoulder,
Giving no thought to authority,
Sold to the discipleship of possibilities.

The knives away and wound bandaged,
I went to the park and sat under an oak to wait
for her call
Among the multitudes of homeless faiths.

Surreptitious Singularity

Don't let a unified field sneak up on you!

Before you know it there's a cosmos pounding,
On the bulkhead of perfect nothingness,
Dark matter and strange matter,
Weak force and strong force,
Pulsars and star hitters up to bat,
Students in basket weaving courses,
Electromagnetism and gravity,
Red giants and interstellar detours,
Quantum uncertainty
Ann Coulter and *Tuesdays With Morey.*

Doesn't it break your heart?
Only in the Third Act, before inflation
Could an independent observer have quipped:
"Finally, a perfect repose for the empirically
minded!"
Before the the inflationary field bought the damn
farm;
So long singularity, and thanks for all the fission.

You Tell That Asshole To Sober Up

I'm not gonna let your imaginary friend knock
me off my feet!
I have one of my own, who
Stands between me and the unmoved mover
Clad in fine threaded silk, blank
Sweet and vernal in blonde tresses
Presenting to me a conspectus of the divine,
And who am I to say she exists, and who are you to say
"Right Thinking?"

All I know is that my interpreter declares a
gorgeous lie
Though yours might sweat crystal meth,
spoonfed
Is another way to take the leap of faith;
I prefer to be an artisan of *agape*
For all I know is imagination,
All I can do is crawl toward nothing,
And treat it like a fresh canvas.

World of War

76 days into my hermitage I dinged to Level 60.

Time for a celebration; I scraped a fetid shirt off the floor

And emerged, astonished, to see a haggard lumberjack squinting, At me

in the bathroom mirror, some kind of warrior succored by

Cheetos and Mountain Dew.

And as I took a respite from the RPG life,

I wondered, just for a second, if I'd been spending too much time in Silverpine forest

but remembered that Ally, "Justified" on the Sentinels server,

who'd run the gamut of insults:

> /taunt
>
> /slap
>
> /spit

On me.

I beat that motherfucker down, warlock on paladin - he'd never have won.

As I emptied a coffee can of my own urine,

I cried out like Garrosh: For the Horde!

You Can Lead a Judas to Living Water, But Only A Psychopathic God Can Make Him Fink

The time of day most precious to Jesus

was the close of the day,

when comets send the portent of apocalypse

or the Enlightenment (oh, shit!)

and the barebacked gaze with the grim-fated,

into the spread of the milky way; shamed.

Sought by sore fingers; desert twilight hugs the
world with gray

Marks of race and, therefore, dignity

Become as the stone of resurrection immovable
and elusive.

Simply to rest in uncertainty, perhaps,

To query lunacy for his heritage,

Or ask when he should commit suicide,

The time most precious to Jesus

was the close of the day.

UnderMensch: An Origins Story

In the hugger-mugger eye of a the Goshawk there
are no heroes.

The men who heaved against the earth itself, in
terms

proscribed by fair weather – Nature's
dispensation -

were foiled by the phalanx of bryophytes

ground to peat by Douglas firs.

Against living deliberately, to the end, none can
prevail,

              and yes, not even Batman.

The superhero is the tiddly wink of pert and
puerile imaginations

For fire concedes only strategic withdrawals

To the criminal impulse swarms well-oiled brawn

And ultimately the Mahatma himself was a
pervert.

And the Undertaker Issued a Bearish Bellow

"But father will be first in heaven?"
ah, a lesson descried from a slave faith
poor little dear, long-staring at the retreating
hearse
fixed in the Procrustean matrix.

IT is a lugubrious liniment for the grieving.
whence comes the bollocks of belief...
Hera's milk splashed through the sky, as a meme
a desiccated placenta, sung 'do *rei* me'

fa, full of grace, first fruits
first last and last shall be first
the first defeat for the credulous youth
that corpse bearer lost it, gave in to mirth

For What She Learned
on father's knee
And what was amended
with an undertaker's bellow.

Eierkopf

For Leah Libresco, on the occasion of her embracing
moha.

We bid you happy tidings as you depart from
vibrance
to the Vatican masturbatorium, where the fronds
are papal blanched,
the ocher soil, the moral low ground, is
historically bedraggled with semen and blood.

You'll meet the frowsy representatives of joy;
We've already seen it - the prodigal feast of the
new kill,
Our ears freshly perceive the haggard bleating of
a Sophoclean twelve.

A squalor in which even Luther, decked in his
anti-Semitic hauberk,
Could not with ardent denial locate Platonic
forms
The bane of Spinoza and denigration of Galileo

Has, curiously, flanked your intellect.
Platonic abstractions trump
The din of anguished screams from *limbus
infantium?* - fucking christ, no!

The holocaust below your nose, *abusi infantes,*
where families burn in Rwandan sanctuaries
the primal cries of millions purified by steel

Perfectly silenced by your rationale: Moral Law.
You cannot genuflect and forget.
From Epicurus's cradle to the knacker's yard for
spoiled intellects

We send you forth with godspeed.

Manure - "En Gogues!"

When through a quaking bog at crest of night
(squiffed)
A footslog that did our four feet press to shrift
an evening's simpered indiscretions
To an ever stone-faced theo-granite;

We did like eclogue idiots
recount to another the fleecing done
in some old Irish distillery at our backs -
What thrift in shirking comestibles said we!
A pittance saved for a pitcher reserved
and placed on our hardwood table with a
welcome stridor
(You remarked ... "much like a *Death* rattle")

shipped it off to the gut to catalyze
a bellyful of coquettish proverbs
of Tetons and quahogs clamped up
tighter than a snare – but we would, we, slither
        and pry:

The intended business shirked, or made of us
shirks
we shifted banter - babies to bravado
the hours slipped
and corporate backbones stiffened
thus, shazam – oh, foibles – at home!

the candles unsnuffed!
Remit our children again

then erring we stepped into the cow patch which,
a day before – the length of a femur – we swore
to flank
but ah, so what, a little shit for a prodigious snit.

Manure – agog!

The Mote In Toast's Eye

Toast was the name, "Beans on" it was given
"hard as" a sobriquet for the women

"Ya gotta swish it with vision," the intake for
each dish kid
noon to ten, Toast on the crack driving his
kitchen

filling the scripts for french fries and chicken
sending out platters of fish or spit vittles

he stayed this side of the looking glass
visage between the "e" and "r" of "diner"

powered by Miller Light and Winston
And a lifetime of friction with "spics"

called them wetbacks and liars
and insisted on black and cracker pearl-divers

but never heard one goddamn emission
of fine old ladies in southern condition:

'that toast, he's a fine cook, a shame he's a
nigger.'

A Tikrit Carol[1]

Complacent at the bottom of the ocean,
Subtle notes, minor chords.
Stuck in a minute's diameter
Briny water gurgles and wordless;
The meadows of the abyss:
Never came home again.

Sunday noontime, sun crowned,
a dubious assurance of clear skies,
Evacuation by the television,
lunch delivered courteously by the microwave,
Suckling the newspaper for pessimism
Vexed by the Catholics home-bound (and stridently).

The kitchen sink iconography:
The tensile power of steely immobility.
A belly full of snakes, or of deepest praise?
Post-church, no depth to sky, lackadaisical on the brink.

---

[1] First published in *The Wick* (Harvard University: Fall 2008) p. 40.

And kindling to get the fire going.

Quarter-to-one;
A knock on the door
A ghost in the eaves

Unchristian blood in the snow, in the desert, in
red states.
Noël, noël for the unbelievers.

Complacent at the bottom of the ocean,
Subtle notes, minor chords.
Stuck in a minute's diameter
Briny water gurgles and wordless;
The meadows of the abyss:
never came home again.

Stars Die

I pray to the sky and observe
Ghosts on platinum trails, in higher cones of time
Whose souls burned out a billion years ago
and know that
stars die.

With tools as straight as swords the poets of the
human time
Made sense in climates ardent and disconsolate
Now banished to damp and crusting pages
I know that
stars die.

I love you now, when life is doubling between us
and you split away
Discharging lightning bolts of blood, and feet like
cold fish
Your fuel and light spent at last
And I know that even
stars die

Gas Station Mercury

I'm awed by her stature when she bends her body
to pump gas.
A flawless example of late summer skin.

"Nice day, isn't it?" I ask.
Somehow, the vibrations reach her ears. She
turns and stands akimbo.

She's wrapped in impossibly tight pink jeans like
a watermelon Jolly Rancher.
She regards me owl-like, florid and impenetrable
atop soaring breasts.

At once I see it again. The Great Wall between
Abercrombie and honesty.
She will squash me like an ant crashing her
beach blanket.

I shift my gaze to her Volkswagen. Whoa, I
almost say out loud when I see it, her saving
grace.
A copy Sexton's *Complete Poems*, striving in the
back seat, back unbroken.

She follows me in to the cash register and when
she pays

My fingers, criminal partners of Exxon
Incorporated, brush softly on her hand.

Thank Zeus, she asks if I could give her a cash
receipt.

I scribble "men kill for this or for as much" on the
back, and with my duty fulfilled, the
messenger flees.

Greg

I was told he always kept a shopping cart in tow,
Stacked top-heavy and to the edges with puzzle pieces,
Winnowed molded plastic, from moldy histories
With his wheels firmly on the tracks
That the rest of us refuse to follow;
An artist needs wheels, a classroom on the go.

His *magnum opus* began with a concrete divider,
A canvas for Santa Monica, the German and Japanese tourists,
His portrait of the hometown
A sculpture hewn from celebrity refuse
Soda cans inserted into orange pylons;
And pigment squeezed from Hollywood and Vine.

No one asked him what he sought,
Or if he wanted a bite to eat, or warmth, or something to read,
He seemed sustained by a long abandoned feeling
Some decadent food from an ancient paradise.

Oblique, the mirror image of context,
An impressionist in a first-impression town.

The day they came down and took him,
There was a freak chill on Venice beach,-
Bearing the blight law as a muzzle
The artless blue took him to stir
His lifework forced into the portrait the city
makes;

The peculiarities brushed into a landfill.
But he'd fingered the sand before his abduction,
In the place where his Pepsi and pylons had
stood,
And left a few words
that were taken by the rain:
"i will, for art."

The Woman Without A Shadow

She walks a path of white sands, flanked by
seagull suitors

She dexterously prepares herself with lipstick
and blush as she goes

She recites elegies to the imagined manatees and
fancied mangroves in a saline mire

She fixes her solitary shell, her handspun and
footloose painter's hat, against the wind;

When she comes, the tiger sharks cower in
rusting hulls along the continental shelf.

Her sparse laughter scores the clement in the air,
a lobster's handshake

Her hands cradle a conch like it is her only child,
but with a kiss it becomes ashes

Her tears are acid that wilts and browns the dune
grass

When she summons her late husband's specter,
her face creases to bear such gravity.

The woman with no shadow is pinned, back faced to
the sun

She cannot escape her Atlantic home, her
Codder's paradise.

The winter tourists take her picture, a curio
beneath a March umbrella

Reading a doctor's note through steel bars.

Then summer comes and the wary locals glare

At the grisly exchange of sand dollars for funeral
flowers,

The living corpse and her desperate economy.

The Dope Flask

       times
when asked
i am, by Knight-Captains of screeds
'just who are you'
       tempted
am i, not by memes
but a flask
that ushers definition

       'i am'
i say
       'the flicked booger.'
on the wall,
       'the succored tick'
on the beggar
       'for poetry'
appurtenance
'is not beauty'
it is
       'pus.'

gangrene

copula
frisson,
there is enough

for those who are quick
for those who are not
      me
i can only produce grit
i am not in that strata
      so drink
      pus
      and be, pus
      is me,
pus.

Sonnet 1 (Face of a Gravestone)

Face of a gravestone in a nameless yard
Hewn from a quarry an unneeded cross
More cold than a prison and rusting bars
Marble museum overgrown with moss
An end unbefitting a human life.
What mem'ry is gleaned from this undead space?
No shrine; bland scripture in sand and lichen
Sow coffins and the life cycle's erased.
Where are the signs that hold my passing still?
Take hand with those that recall and still cry
The line of a smile is my lasting will
Reposed with friends my enduring soul lies.
Face of a gravestone? Remember my face.
Smile back when you come to my resting place.

Sonnet 2 (Schooled In)

There were twenty-one logical reasons,
To heed the trees those three weeks into March,
Learnèd evergreens schooled in hopelessly,
Attend to wasting disease in their bark.
Endangered birds keeping hope in numbers
Forage for songs; owls in humble lookouts
Listen hard for an echo to return
And a porcupine sends down hemlock scouts.
'Neath a sturdy shield of ice, fish await,
In suspense, a new feat of chemistry.
The cubs and does will brave a hunter's bait
While squirrels sort plastic from acorn seeds.
Watching o'er the miserables, the rain
Dowses trees, licked fingers hoping some change.

Sonnet 3 (Yellow House)

Out of the blue came burden to people
Living in a yellow house. Someone played
With shadows, someone broke a solemn creed
And left behind a candy coated cleft.
It regards you like a defiant smile.
A bucket and scrawny cats strain to hear
What chipped paint and garden tools left outside
In winter declare so eloquently.
The windswept yard harbors a biblical
Lamentation, a dolor mourning the
Black mistakes painted over with blonde fill;
A case of fence posts where milestones should be,
Like a breath of snow going out the gate,
Like a yellow house unconsummated.

Sonnet 4 (Inoculate, or Pray?)

A choice – born once or born captious?
The doctrine goes out to torpid storm clouds
While I don a Cosmic hero's passing.
"Are you sorry too?" I wonder aloud
And the demon-haunted world all around
Doomed now, over later, to die in shame
And quaintly watch the first snowflake down
With a kindred sense of welcome outstayed.
In cloisters, holding heat as tarmac does,
Clergymen find six and six now make nine
Take bravery in standing tall above
Sacrifices on lukewarm ground divine.
I shout "in the wilderness!" but none hear,
Choke up, kneel down and count the frozen tears.

Sonnet 5 (The Hooker)

She became a hooker progressively
From a wino's sordid fingers into
The mail man's fishy pocket, change heavy
for buying a make-up rose. and then quick
to the schoolboy's rucksack, laden with coy
letters penned when the teacher didn't see
to break misogyny from stir, the ploy -
is it chivalry, or equality?
and to the policeman itching to frisk
the mold that makes men as a tabby cat
the privilege that makes fists of whiskers
Or a shadow on the magazine rack?
But she's a hooker, still, and we adore
Her honesty, her feet, and nothing more.

After the 2004 Election

Four hours have passed on the fried-chicken-
slick highway,

The driver seat honey gummy with heat sweat,

Me, smiling, like the drive were an amusement
park ride;

Ticked off by moments of *satori* in the
underpasses,

Homeless folk making cave painting shadows in a
Cro-Magnon halogen light,

Then, crossing, I raise a lonely finger salute and
cry: Take this, Dixie! –

There are mysteries in stands of New England
forest,

Beyond the clear cut turnpike borders like
exposed bone.

The river Styx would not have been so
formidable,

If it stood between the Mason Dixon line and
Maine lobster,

Heck no, I'd have paid a gold coin per eye or
more to lock my jaw on,

Soft shelled crabs, pancakes with Vermont pure.

I couldn't expound in the marshes of the
Southern swamp.

You've got your honor, and good for you,

But I perceived – call me fatally Yankee –

A perishing pride beneath the southern
Hospitality,

Something like the plaintive look of a
confessioner,

You just couldn't mask behind that good ol' boy
soteriology.

I admit, it wasn't a catharsis transcending from
red to blue

When I crossed the state line into Maryland, you
see,

Nothing is so simple. We've got a faith here too,

Constructed of taboos absolved from their
turmoil,

You could call it godlessness, and be
incrementally correct

I guess I'd call it punctuated equilibrium (as
opposed to the unchallenged kind)

Or more plainly, the interjection of ass-freezing
winters every year.

Must be something in the cold that disrupts decorum,

And one starts asking questions of tradition;

Not quite Emily Post, I realize. Here we are, even so,

Cold assed iconoclasts, noses turned up in pretension

Casting lots with Catholics and buggering Nutmeggers.

Under duress, I'd have to confess that there's grace in every place,

Of course, a boon to shifting away from "us and them,"

Even the southern Jesus would agree we're all brothers and sisters.

I can only be honest: I adore foliage and Katahdin,

And, though the parking appalls, likewise Boston;

I've made my getaway from Flatland, and I don't think I'll ever miss it.

Gravity, Defined

happiness is placement
the arrangement of space matters-,
outside the door of the hospital
where asphalt ice-crusted
and bleak sunlight make headway
i would be
down.

here,
it is another kind of matter-,
there are mental health geomancers
who have provided feng shui for my cortex
i am well, all is well
since things are pinned down
and i cannot lift a bottle or a knife

Well love, that's mere art
a lie for telling some truth
but i have this scrap of thanks

you gave me love
you gave me
gravity

Metaphysics of the Intolerable

kristin is in spiral galaxy rotation
Embracing collision with sardonic faces
her charity digressing, my celerity erasing
A sibilant ending for time and space.

She's superposition ecstasy, to me.
A parallel brane, and shared brains too
AND syncopation: silver fish in morning whirlpools
her chary expressions strike me jejune.

I want to rescue her.
I wonder what to do about the relationship
To put us on the dole, or not,
I consider both strings and the multiverse -

But will it help, the anthropic principle in love?
Fucking introductions! barbarians to spacemen -
to declare "i love you" in ape or astrophysicist
is still to gainsay the metaphysics of the intolerable.

Eggshells & Entropy

one can cavil the words of a learn'd astronomer
but she still hits the mark perfectly:
with you, kristin, the gain is exponential
i want three years to a trillion,
i cannot let entropy win.

Organic Garden Abracadabra

Something there is that loves seeding
Supposing that tomatoes are so easy
It makes a wonder of the mind -
steel corridors, patrolled by white coated
farmers.
that which is salubrious for the body
is a miracle to the mind, that is the
wager of organic gardening...
but woe, that those modified minds
make GMOs and therefore more food
                    for more people
The sod of Walden heaves with outrage
tossing patchouli eco-warriors into a fitful compost.

Fuck You Boots
(Size 6, Black Leather)

the discovery of radium and a double helix
made mockeries of male privilege
      but

Christ, there's a vulture pecking at her heels
and those [boots] are an expensive brand (Benign
Sexism)!
from sidewalk to sidewalk and sidling along
with the assumption of chivalry: no: no.

'i'm self-made and shimmering aerial,'
              she says
'a willing idiot and a flat tire'
              the [duo] rejoins

and men are left inchoate
but there is an exit to dignity
don't hold the door or pick up the tab

but shout out, over learned stupidity: no, no.

fuck you [boots]
and fuck you vapid [cunt].

Flesh Flash Mob

a flash mob is a burst of art
for timid makers well-intending
likewise, a very public fart
for both break entitlement

remind the world of chaos
lurking 'round a ficus tree
offend for making plain the cost
sickles, suckling, serendipity.

all at once the rotunda is filled with cocks
a flesh flash mob?
tits and ass and argyle socks
more timely than a suicide bomber!

Heart Beat, Pig Meat, First Tweet

'bacon is the best'
I jump on two fads at once
a cat Instagram

Cold Feet, Effete, Second Tweet

none follow me since
my poor review: eat, pray, love
'selfish, whiny bitch'

Troll Meet, Leetspeak, Account Delete

'lol ur gay'
gives me pause – social networks?
word rape/Heidegger

Ally[2]

there's a Witness at the door
knock, knock, knock

a lip-glossy serves my
Dunkin'
twat, twat, twat

the Homeland reads my blog
cha, cha, cha!

the one percent shits in my
mouth
ca, ca, ca

but a queer guy who said 'i get you'
is who i'm supposed to hate.

Fah, fah, fuck that.

---

[2]Based on the rhythm of a Ugandan call and response song.

Do Archbishops Dream of Altar Boy's Feet?

At Wal-Mart this morning, Herman overheard:
"Everyone has a rape fantasy, and I don't mean just men."
Now that was a curious asseveration, he thought
and was overcome with a desire to write a proof
with three axioms.

Now that is chopped up prose, he thought.
So I will frame my fearful verses lyrically:
"One cannot determine from is what one ought,"
came the first, "instinct compels to procreate," secondly

and last, "consent is annulled if free will is a lie,"
thus, arguably, rape is not a fantasy, nor even a sin
and thence, I believe, the crime is believing that I
have any choice about waiting - or how shall I begin?

Metacognition. "Je pense, donc je suis," a thought *á la Cartes*

But if I am, and if through being I am under duress
it is also true "je pense, donc je dois faire foutre,"
an Act of Religion, "je dois accepter Foucault."

Then spying a couple from Saturday mass
He quickly assumed the mantle of piety
and sequestered his treatise on altar boy's asses
as viceroy of the pederast psychopath deity.

About the Author

Born in Willimantic, Connecticut, Jace Paul began his life in crushing indigence, a precocious boy in a broken home. Despite social maladjustment he held forth through public schooling and became an academically successful student. He began writing at age thirteen. While a student at the University of Connecticut, he founded The Poetry Society and moonlighted in classes on acting, directing, French, and philosophy - none of which were pertinent to his behavioral neuroscience major. Upon graduating, Paul worked as a research assistance in the Laboratory of Visual Neuroscience, but later left research over his objections to the use of animals in experimental design. In 2004, he entered Andover-Newton Theological School to study ministry, but later changed course to take up religious studies. In 2009 - 2010 he went to Harvard University, ostensibly to study theology but once again moonlighting in as many other unrelated courses as he could get away with taking.

Paul resides in eastern Connecticut's "quiet corner," where he continues to write and direct independent films.

Visit: http://www.jacepaul.com

CPSIA information can be obtained
at www.ICGtesting.com
Printed in the USA
LVHW052154180520
655844LV00004B/445